Theo von Taane

Minecraft
Notebook
„Ender Dragon"

Between author of this book and producers of Minecraft or one of its subsidiaries is no connection. This book is neither approved or supported by Minecraft nor of one of its subsidiaries and furthermore in any way connected with this parties.

Bibliografische Information der Deutschen Nationalbibliothek:
Die Deutsche Nationalbibliothek verzeichnet diese Publikation in der Deutschen Nationalbibliografie; detaillierte bibliografische Daten sind im Internet über http://dnb.dnb.de abrufbar.

© 2016 Theo von Taane; 1. Auflage
Covergraphic & illustrations © Theo von Taane

Herstellung und Verlag: BoD – Books on Demand, Norderstedt

ISBN: 9783739228761

Books of Theo von Taane

book	ISBN / order nr.
Football note- and tactic book	9783734749605
Badminton note- and tactic book	9783734749643
Baseball note- and tactic book	9783734749650
Basketball note- and tactic book	9783734749681
Bowling note- and tactic book	9783734749698
Cricket note- and tactic book	9783734749711
Ice Hockey note- and tactic book	9783734749728
Fencing note- and tactic book	9783734749735
Field Hockey note- and tactic book	9783734749810
Football (Soccer) note- and tactic book	9783734749827
Futsal note- and tactic book	9783734749834
Handball note- and tactic book	9783734749841
Lacrosse Women note- and tactic book	9783734749858
Lacrosse Men note- and tactic book	9783734749865
Netball note- and tactic book	9783734749872
Rugby note- and tactic book	9783734749889
Chess note- and tactic book	9783734749896
Squash note- and tactic book	9783734749902
Tennis note- and tactic book	9783734749919
Table Tennis note- and tactic book	9783734749926
Volleyball note- and tactic book	9783734749933
Water Polo note- and tactic book	9783734749940

Majestic Flowers and Butterflies
- Adult Coloring Book - ISBN: 9783739227085

This coloring book for adults contains 36 beautiful patterns of various flowers. Experience hours full of stress relief, mindful calm, creative expression and fun.

Use crayons, felt-tip pens and colored pencils to give the patterns a personal touch.

Millions of people worldwide have rediscovered the simple relaxation and joy of coloring!

Join this community and find yourself enchanted by the magical passion of inspiring coloring.